A BLUE Poetry PAINTBOX

Chosen by John Foster

Oxford University Press

Oxford University Press, Walton Street, Oxford OX2 6DP

Oxford New York Toronto
Delhi Bombay Calcutta Madras Karachi
Kuala Lumpur Singapore Hong Kong Tokyo
Nairobi Dar es Salaam Cape Town
Melbourne Auckland Madrid

and associated companies in
Berlin Ibadan

First Published in paperback 1994
First published in hardback 1994

A CIP catalogue record for this book is available from the British Library

Illustrations by

Rowan Barnes-Murphy, Bucket, Frances Cony, Andy Cooke,
Paul Downling, Peet Ellison, Rhian Nest James, Sally Kilroy,
Jan Lewis, Valerie McBride, Alan Marks, Jill Newton,
David Parkins, Korky Paul, Valeria Petrone, Mary Price-Jenkins,
Jessica Richardson-Jones, Graham Round, Meg Rutherford, Caroline Sharpe,
Martin Ursell, Jenny Williams, Joe Wright.

ISBN 0 19 916679 X (paperback)
ISBN 0 19 916720 6 (hardback)

Printed in Hong Kong

Contents

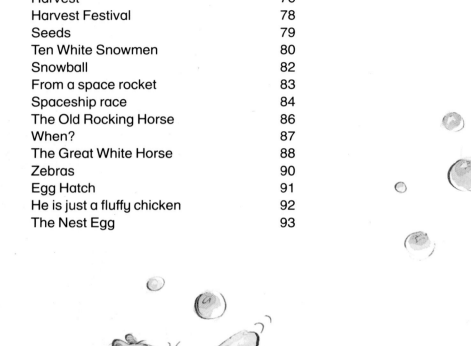

There was an old pirate

There was an old pirate called Pete
Who captured a whole fishing fleet.
He said 'Don't be scared,
All your lives will be spared.
I only want something to eat!'

Wendy Larmont

I wish I was a pirate

I wish I was a pirate
   With a long beard hanging down,
A cutlass dangling from my belt,
   My teeth all black and brown.

A parrot on my shoulder.
   A patch upon one eye,
A pirate ship to sail on,
   A pirate flag to fly.

The rolling waves would be my home,
   I'd live through many wrecks.
I'd always have the best of maps –
   The one's marked with an X!

Pirates don't have parents,
   They don't get sent to school.
They never have to take a bath,
   For them there are no rules.

Yo-ho-ho me hearties!
   It's a pirate's life for me . . .
Pistols in my pockets,
   Salt-pork for my tea!

Tony Bradman

Snip the Sneak

I'm reading a book about smugglers
And the exciting things they did,
About the goods that they smuggled
And the caves in which they hid.

I think I'd be a good smuggler
For I could sneak in and out,
I could sneak up and sneak down,
I could creep and crawl about.

I'm going to look in the papers
Where they advertise each week.
I'm going to become a smuggler.
I'll be known as Snip the Sneak.

John Rice and John Foster

WANTED... SMUGGLERS

No experience necessary. Long trips abroad. No pets (except parrots). Excellent money to be made. Applicants must not be afraid of customs men or high waves.

Apply on parchment to
Jack 'The Keg' Kingston
The Hawkhurst Gang
near the beach
Kent.

9

Dear Mr Merlin

Could you fix it for me
to be a wizard for the day?
Please send an invitation —
I'd love to come and stay.

I'll get all the proper gear,
black cloak and pointed hat,
sprinkle them with star-shapes
and bring my own pet bat.

If I can be your assistant
I'll work hard all day long.
I'll stir the simmering cauldron
till spells are hot and strong.

10

I'll gladly add in eyes of
newts and spiders by the load
if you can fix a recipe to
turn my brother into a toad.

You're a modern man, Mr Merlin,
I know you couldn't care less
that I'm not some ambitious boy
but an apprentice *wizardess*.

love from
Lucy xxx

Moira Andrew

11

Meddling muddle

'Don't touch that Magic Spell Book!'
The wizard warned the boy.
'Just get on with the sweeping,
I'm off to see King Roy.'

The wizard left the workshop.
The boy rushed up the stair.
He rummaged through the bookcase
And found the spellbook there.

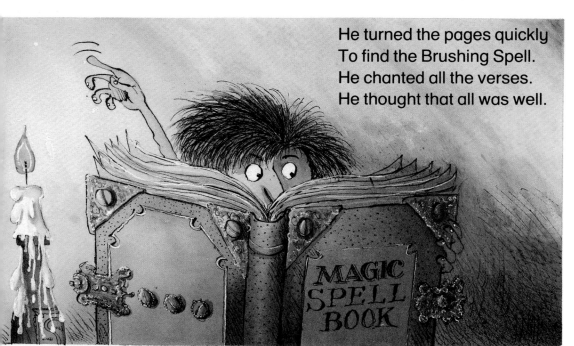

He turned the pages quickly
To find the Brushing Spell.
He chanted all the verses.
He thought that all was well.

And then he started shrinking!
He got a dreadful fright.
He'd cast the spell so quickly
He hadn't said it right.

The wizard came back later.
He peered round the door.
The boy had disappeared.
A mouse was on the floor.

'You foolish little creature!
You've meddled with my book.
I'll have to turn you back again.
Now. Let me take a look.'

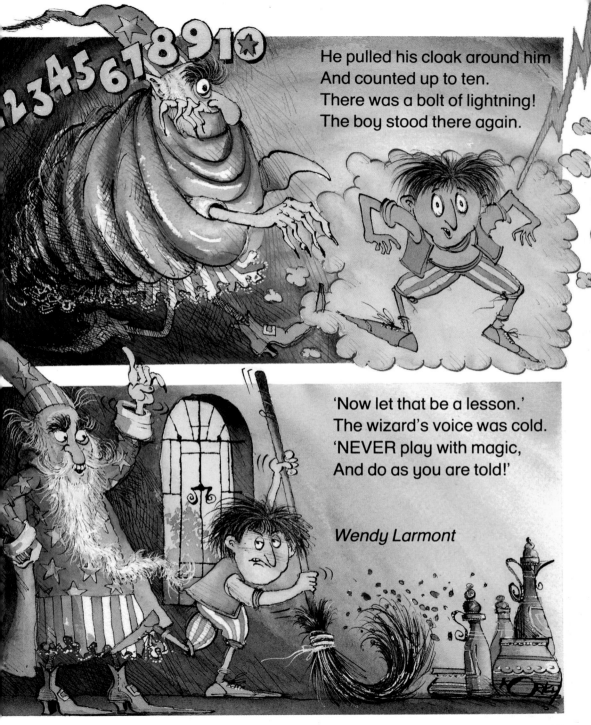

He pulled his cloak around him
And counted up to ten.
There was a bolt of lightning!
The boy stood there again.

'Now let that be a lesson.'
The wizard's voice was cold.
'NEVER play with magic,
And do as you are told!'

Wendy Larmont

The sea-monster's snack

Deep down upon his sandy bed
the monster turned his slimy head,
grinned and licked his salty lips
and ate another bag of ships.

Charles Thomson

Happynessy

Monster Nessy in the Loch,
Sleeps inside a cave of rock.
She swims around and round all day.
It seems a lonely way to play.

So when the tourists stand and stare
She pops her head up in the air.
They gasp and take a photograph,
And monster Nessie starts to laugh.

She quickly dives and hides below.
Is she real? They'll never know!

Wendy Larmont

17

The mermaid

A mermaid sat
On a sandy rock,
And her eyes gleamed soft and green,
'Come with me,' she called,
'And I'll take you away
To the land beneath the sea.'

'We'll ride on a dolphin,
We'll tickle a whale,
Eat seaweed cake for our tea,'
And she held out her hand
As she dived through the waves,
'Come with me
      Come with me
            Come with me.'

Theresa Heine

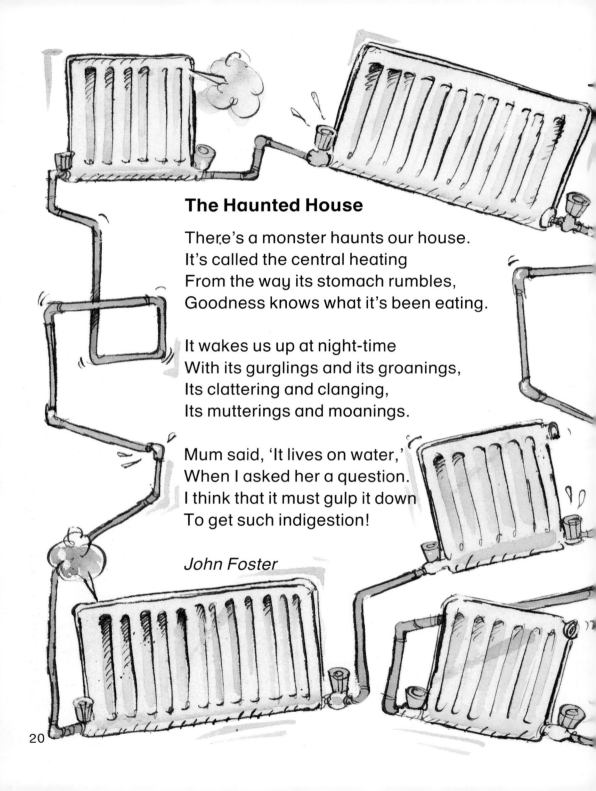

The Haunted House

There's a monster haunts our house.
It's called the central heating
From the way its stomach rumbles,
Goodness knows what it's been eating.

It wakes us up at night-time
With its gurglings and its groanings,
Its clattering and clanging,
Its mutterings and moanings.

Mum said, 'It lives on water,'
When I asked her a question.
I think that it must gulp it down
To get such indigestion!

John Foster

The Shadow Man

At night-time
As I climb the stair
I tell myself
There's nobody there.

But what if there is?
What if he's there —
The Shadow Man
At the top of the stair?

What if he's lurking
There in the gloom
Of the landing
Right outside my room?

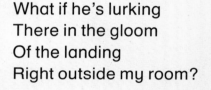

The Shadow Man
Who's so hard to see
What if he's up there
Waiting for me?

At night-time
As I climb the stair
I tell myself
There's nobody there.

John Foster

Ghostly Lessons

Mum, I want some chocolate,
just one little treat —
peppermint or strawberry cream . . .

GHOSTS DON'T EAT!

Mum, I've got a toothache,
a pain beneath my heel;
my throat's too sore to work tonight. . .

GHOSTS DON'T FEEL!

Mum, I really hate the dark —
I hate the way they stared!
I'm scared of graveyards, woods and folk . . .

GHOSTS AREN'T SCARED!

Judith Nicholls

Who's Afraid?

Do I have to go haunting tonight?
The children might give me a fright.
It's dark in that house.
I might meet a mouse.
Do I have to go haunting tonight?

I don't like the way they scream out,
When they see me drifting about.
I'd much rather stay here,
Where there's nothing to fear.
Do I have to go haunting tonight?

John Foster

25

The castle

I love the castle
On the hill;
When I'm there
Time stands still.

I walk around
The ruined walls,
Then wait inside
The ancient hall.

It has no roof,
But soon I hear
Something from
Across the years.

Knights and ladies,
Barking dogs,
Jesters joking,
Crackling logs.

Neighing horses,
Clash of steel,
Battle raging;
It's so *real*.

When I'm there
I might believe . . .
But no, it can't be.
Time to leave.

Tony Bradman

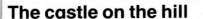

The castle on the hill

On the hill there is a castle.
Round the castle there is a moat.
Over the moat there is a bridge.
Beyond the bridge there is a door.
Through the door there is a courtyard.
Across the courtyard there stands a tower.
Inside the tower there is a staircase.
Up the staircase there is a door.
Across the door iron bolts are drawn.
Behind the door a young girl sleeps . . .

On the hill there stands a castle.
Round the castle there is a moat . . .

John Foster

A song of sevens

Once there was a castle
with seven doors
and each of the doors
had seven locks
and each of the locks
had seven keys
and the doors were locked up tight.

Inside the castle
were seven princesses
and each princess
had seven maids
and each of the maids
knew seven songs
and they sang them every night.

One day to the castle
came seven princes
and each of the princes
brought seven servants
and each of the servants
had seven swords
and the swords were shining bright.

They hacked the locks
of the seven doors
and each of the locks
gave seven creaks
and each of the doors
gave seven groans
and the castle was filled with light.

They rode away
with the seven princesses
and each of the princes
married his princess
and each of the servants
wed one of the maids
at a wedding feast full of delight.

Irene Rawnsley

St. George and the Dragon

St. George looked at the dragon
And much to his surprise,
He noticed that the dragon
Had large appealing eyes.
'Pardon me,' said brave St. George,
'I hear you're cruel and sly.'
'Oh no, not me,' the dragon said,
'I wouldn't hurt a fly.'
'I've come to slay you,' said St. George,
'And save the maiden fair
That you have captured, and no doubt
Imprisoned in your lair.'
'I used to be both cruel and sly,
Of that there is no doubt,'
Replied the dragon, 'but not now,
My fire has all burnt out.
The maiden you have come to save
Has made a pet of me.
She takes me walkies on a lead
And feeds me cups of tea.
So if you want to do brave deeds
The like of which I've read,
Please take the maiden home with you,
And so save me instead.'

Finola Akister

32

The Sleepy Dragon

A dragon awoke
in his mountain lair
where he'd slept
for a thousand years.

His treasure was rusty
his scales were dusty
his throat was dry
his wings wouldn't fly
his throat was croaky
his fire was smoky
his eyes weren't flashing
his tail wasn't lashing
his claws couldn't scratch
though he tried.

So he sighed
and stretched himself
over the floor
and went back to sleep
for a thousand years more.

Irene Rawnsley

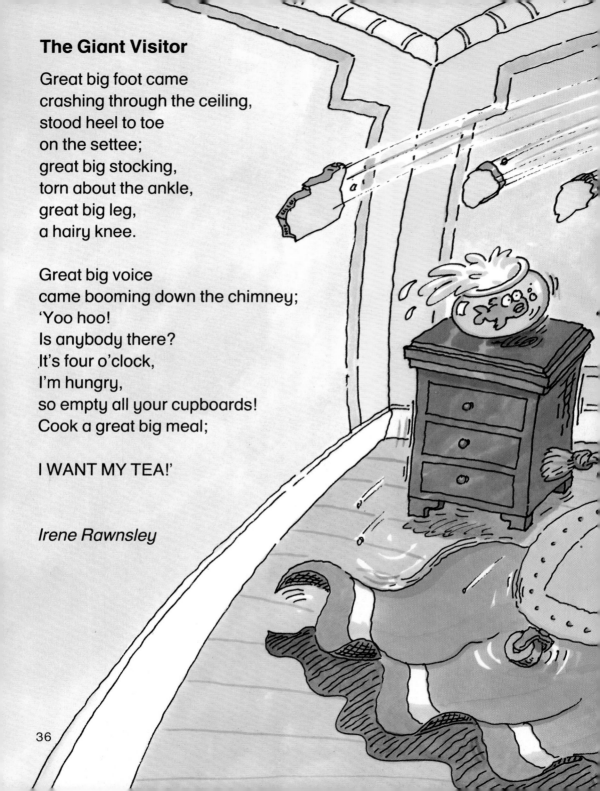

The Giant Visitor

Great big foot came
crashing through the ceiling,
stood heel to toe
on the settee;
great big stocking,
torn about the ankle,
great big leg,
a hairy knee.

Great big voice
came booming down the chimney;
'Yoo hoo!
Is anybody there?
It's four o'clock,
I'm hungry,
so empty all your cupboards!
Cook a great big meal;

I WANT MY TEA!'

Irene Rawnsley

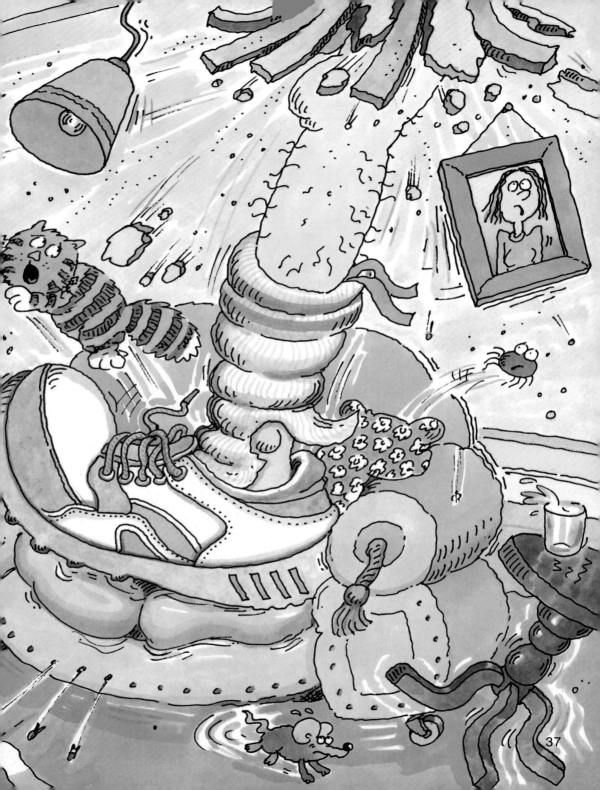

Giant Tale

He was . . .

As wide as an oak tree,
tall as a willow;
his snore was the thunder,
a mountain his pillow.

Each step brought an earthquake,
each breath blew a gale;
one laugh moved an ocean,
each tear filled a pail.

His mouth was a crater,
with snakes for a tongue;
his eyes were the size
of the earth and the sun.

One toe was as heavy
as Venus and Mars;
his forehead was Saturn,
his hair shone with stars.

Judith Nicholls

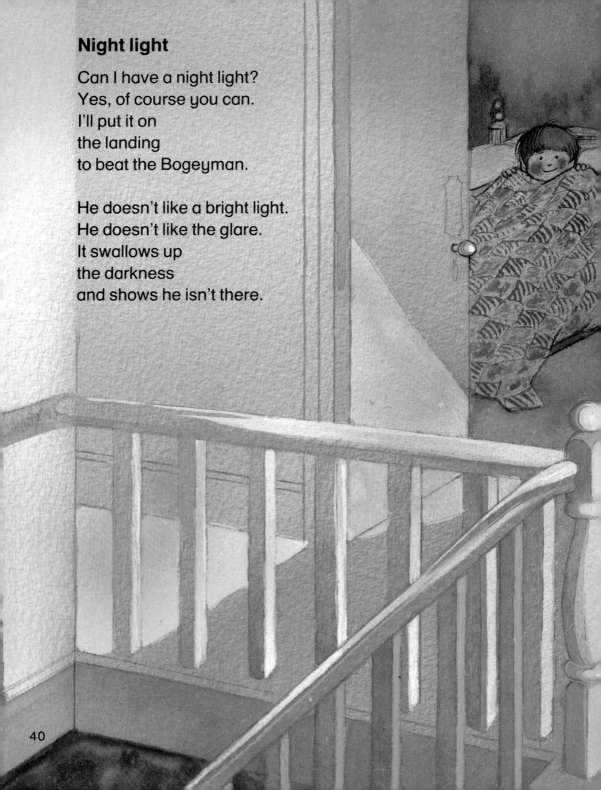

Night light

Can I have a night light?
Yes, of course you can.
I'll put it on
the landing
to beat the Bogeyman.

He doesn't like a bright light.
He doesn't like the glare.
It swallows up
the darkness
and shows he isn't there.

40

You can have a night light
burning bright and strong
to drive away
the darkness
all night long.

Jean Kenward

41

Midnight visitors

Hedgehog comes snuffing
in his prickly coat,
scuffing the leaves for slugs.

Cat comes soft as a moth,
a shadow painted on the lawn
by moonlight.

Owl comes floating,
sits still as a cat on the wall,
watching, listening.

Mouse freezes under the leaves
on tiptoe paws,
quick eyes pin-bright,
hungry.

Irene Rawnsley

43

At the seaside

I walked on the beach
in my brand new clothes
and stood on the sand
at the edge of the sea
and the sun was shining, shining.

I stepped to the water
on slippery stones
in my brand new shoes
to search for crabs
in the rock pools shining, shining.

A big wave spilled
and toppled me
in my brand new clothes
to the cold wet sea
with the pebbles shining, shining.

They brought me home
in my wet-through clothes
to my tucked-up bed
with a brand new cold
and a sore nose shining, shining.

Irene Rawnsley

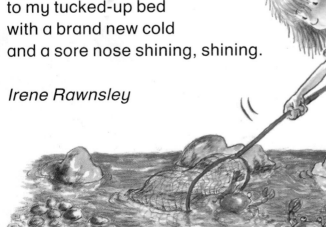

45

Pebbles

I pull the pebble from the sand
And hold the pebble in my hand.
It feels so smooth and cool and old.
I dream the stories it's been told —
Of princes travelled from distant lands,
Of pirates roaming in fierce bands,
Of mighty fighting fish and whales,
Of savage storms and wrecking gales,
Of dead men drowned that tell no tales,
Of battleships, of love, of hate,
Of fisher-wives who wait and wait.
A million pebbles on the beach
And each its different tale to teach.

John Kitching

The Shell

In winter I put a shell to my ear
And through it I hear
The sound of the sea
Answer me.

'Are the donkey and funfair,
Boats and gulls still there?
The pier wading out from the land
And starfish like badges on the sand
Will they be there when I come next year?'
The whispering tide
In the shell replies,
'They will all be here
When you come next year.'

Stanley Cook

The Christmas star

A star looked down
from the frosty sky,
saw three lost Kings
and winked its eye.

'Follow me,' it said
and blazed a trail
over sand and plain,
up-hill, down-dale.

It stopped at Bethlehem
above a poor shed.
'Here?' asked the Kings.
'The Child has no bed.'

'Here,' said the star
and faded from sight,
as sun bathed the Baby
in clear morning light.

Moira Andrew

Star fish

Star fish Star fish
Sparkling white,
Did you fall out of the night?
Were you once a star above,
Come to see the earth you love?
To see the people here below
To let them touch you, so they know,
That there are stars inside the sea
That stars are just like you and me,
That there are stars along the beach
Beneath our feet, within our reach?
Star fish Star fish
Sparkling white
Did you fall out of the night?

Clive Riche

The Fox and the Crow

A farmer's wife threw out some cheese,
and before you could count three,
A crow swooped down and carried it off
to the top branch of a tree.

All this was seen by a hungry fox,
who called up to the crow:
'How *very* beautiful you are!
Has no one told you so?'

Now since the crow still held the cheese
quite firmly in his beak,
He gave a nod to the fox below,
but didn't dare to speak.

'Not only are you beautiful,'
the fox said, 'but I've heard
your voice is lovelier than the voice
of any other bird!'

The crow, puffed up by all of this,
    smiled down at the fox below,
But his beak still firmly held the cheese
    and did not let it go.

'If I could hear your song,' said the fox,
    'I'd soon be able to tell
if it's true that even the nightingale
    cannot sing half as well!'

At once, the crow broke into song –
    a single, ugly 'Caw' –
And the cheese fell from his open mouth
    on to the forest floor.

The fox, quick as lightning, snapped it up
    and laughed to think such a prize
Could be won from a crow stupid enough
    to fall for a pack of lies!

Raymond Wilson   53

The Corn Scratch Kwa Kwa Hen and the Fox

And the Corn Scratch Kwa Kwa Hen
Heard the grumbling rumbling belly
Of the Slink Back Brush Tail Fox
A whole field away.

And she said to her sisters in the henhouse,
'Sisters, that Slink Back Brush Tail Fox
Will come and here's what we must do,'
And she whispered in their sharp sharp ears, 'kwa kwa.'

And when that Slink Back Brush Tail Fox
Came over the field at night,
She heard his paw slide on a leaf,
And the Corn Scratch Kwa Kwa Hen and her sisters
Opened their beaks and —

'KWA!'
The moon jumped
And the Chooky Chook Chicks
Hid under the straw and giggled,
It was the **LOUDEST KWA** in the world.

And the Log Dog and the Scat Cat
And the Brat Rat and the House Mouse
And the Don't Harm Her Farmer
And his Life Wife and their Shorter Daughter
And their One Son came running,

On their slip slop, flip flop,
Scatter clatter, slick flick, tickly feet
And they opened their mouths and shouted –

'FOX!'
And it was the **LOUDEST NAME** in the world.
And the Slink Back Brush Tail Fox
Ran over the fields and far away
And hid in a hole with his grumbling rumbling belly.

And the Corn Scratch Kwa Kwa Hen
Tucked the Chooky Chook Chicks under her feathers
And said 'kwa,'
And it was the softest kwa in the world.

Julie Holder

In the middle of the night

In the middle of the night,
While we slept,
The mouse crept
Out of the nest
Beneath the floor boards.

In the middle of the night,
While everything was quiet,
The mouse scampered
Across the kitchen floor
Searching for breadcrumbs.

In the middle of the night
While Mum and Dad slept
I crept
Quietly down the stairs
To get myself a drink.

In the middle of the night
When I opened the door
Of the kitchen
I saw a flash of fur
As a small brown mouse
Shot past me.

And I jumped with fright
In the middle of the night.

John Foster

59

Jenny Williams 19.

A Mouse in the Kitchen

There's a mouse in the kitchen
    Playing skittles with the peas,
He's drinking mugs of coffee
    And eating last week's cheese.

There's a mouse in the kitchen
    We could catch him in a hat,
Otherwise he'll toast the teacakes
    And that's bound to annoy the cat.

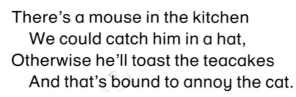

There's a mouse in the kitchen
    Ignoring all our wishes,
He's eaten tomorrow's dinner
    But at least he's washed the dishes.

John Rice

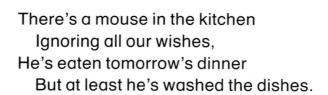

Monkey babies

Don't leave your monkey baby
sitting by the swamp;
a crocodile might eat him.
Chomp! Chomp! Chomp!

Don't leave your monkey baby
sitting under the trees;
a snake might wrap him up.
Squeeze! Squeeze! Squeeze!

Don't leave your monkey baby
sitting by the track;
a lion might be lurking.
Snack! Snack! Snack!

Keep your monkey baby
high up in the trees.
Feed him on bananas.
Help pick off his fleas.

Irene Rawnsley and John Foster

You little monkey!

My mum said
I was behaving
like a little monkey.

So I climbed
onto the sofa
and started swinging
on the door.

When she told me to stop,
I made chattering noises
and pretended
to scratch my armpits.

I refused
to talk properly
until tea-time,
when all I got
was a plate of nuts
and a banana!

So I decided
To stop
Monkeying about.

John Foster

My dad's a gorilla

My dad's a gorilla when he gets mad,
He starts to rant and roar.
Then walks about on his hands and knees,
And rolls around the floor.
He's also very hairy,
Hairs poke out through his vest,
And like a real gorilla
He stands and thumps his chest.

Martin Honeysett

The Flying Reptiles Race

Five flying reptiles were just about to dine.
The dinner had arrived and it looked just fine.
Then up jumped a bossy one and shouted with glee,
'I bet that I could beat you to the Far-Away Tree!'

The other reptiles laughed and they cried, 'No way!
We're the fastest in the land, we could beat you any day!'
The bossy one boasted, 'I am the fastest one!'
But they all disagreed. So the race was on.

They lined up on the cliff edge ready to begin.
Five flying reptiles each saying, 'I'll win!'
They gazed across the ocean stretching far beyond the sand.
'The winner,' said the bossy one, 'is first back to land.'

Then 'Go!' screeched the bossy one giving them a fright –
And four foolish reptiles flew off into the night.
One bossy greedy reptile went off alone to dine,
'They won't be back till dawn,' he said, 'the dinner is all mine!'

Irene Yates

The Wheelchair Race

We were side by side in the corridor,
trying to pass the time,
talking about what we both enjoyed,
his chair parked next to mine.

He showed me how well he whistled.
I told him my drawing was ace.
He asked how fast I could move.
I forget who suggested a race!

He counted us down to zero.
'No dirty tricks,' I said.
We sped along the polished floor.
I made the turn ahead.

We narrowly missed two cleaning ladies,
a nurse and an angry queue,
then knocked a tea trolley sideways,
'Look out, it's the terrible two!'

Our doctor stepped out of his room
to check the dreadful din,
'You might have hurt yourselves,' he said,
but smiled as we wheeled ourselves in.

Brian Moses

I'm a . . .
look-alike
hair-alike
play-alike
share-alike

eat-alike
drink-alike
speak-alike
think-alike

sing-alike
scream-alike
laugh-alike
dream-alike

joke-alike
cook-alike
TALK-ALIKE

LOOK

Me too!

Jud

...like
(...in voices)

I'm a ...
look-alike
hair-alike
play-alike
share-alike

eat-alike
drink-alike
speak-alike
think-alike

sing-alike
scream-alike
laugh-alike
dream-alike

joke-alike
cook-alike
TALK-ALIKE

...E TWIN!

Me too!

...cholls

Reflections

I look in the mirror
And what do I see?
I see my twin sister.
She's looking at me.

We both look the same
In the clothes that we wear.
The same colour eyes
And the same colour hair.

I look in the mirror
And what do I see?
It's not my twin sister.
I'm looking at me.

Wendy Larmont

The Magic Seeds

There was an old woman who sowed a corn seed,
And from it there sprouted a tall yellow weed.
She planted the seeds of the tall yellow flower,
And up sprang a blue one in less than an hour.
The seed of the blue one she sowed in a bed,
And up sprang a tall tree with blossoms of red.
And high in the tree-top there sang a white bird,
And his song was the sweetest that ever was heard.
The people they came from far and near,
The song of the little white bird to hear.

James Reeves

Harvest

Come and see
    the harvest,
come and pick
    the corn!
Make a dolly
    out of it,
one that's quickly
    born.
Turn her arms
    and twist her,
tie her
    here and there.
Now she's like
    a person,
with bright golden
    hair.

Thank you
     for the harvest,
thank you
     for the crop.
We will make
     a loaf of bread
with crust upon
     the top.
Here we come
     a-dancing
with a basket
     full of bread.
Come and see
     our dolly
with a crown
     upon her head!

Jean Kenward

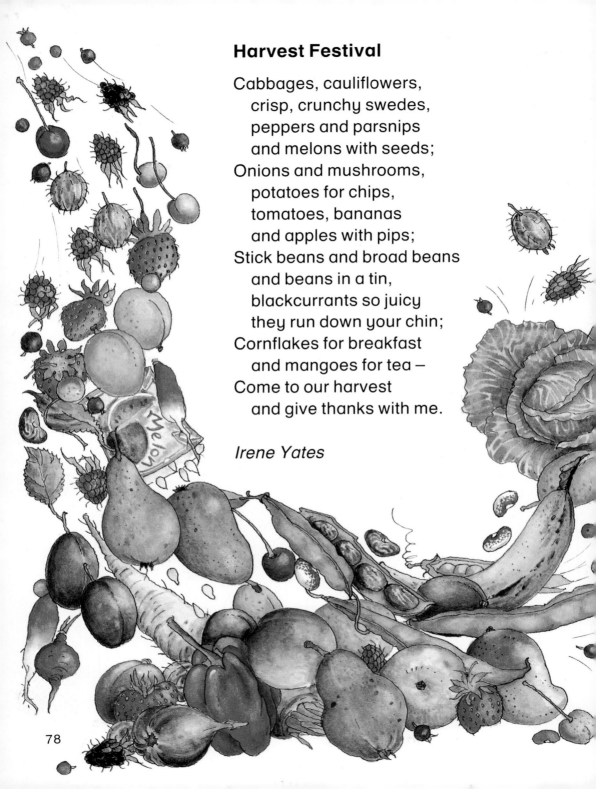

Harvest Festival

Cabbages, cauliflowers,
    crisp, crunchy swedes,
    peppers and parsnips
    and melons with seeds;
Onions and mushrooms,
    potatoes for chips,
    tomatoes, bananas
    and apples with pips;
Stick beans and broad beans
    and beans in a tin,
    blackcurrants so juicy
    they run down your chin;
Cornflakes for breakfast
    and mangoes for tea —
Come to our harvest
    and give thanks with me.

Irene Yates

Seeds

Seeds that twist and seeds that twirl
Seeds with wings which spin and whirl;

Seeds that float on thistledown
Seeds in coats of glossy brown;

Seeds that burst with popping sound
From their pods to reach the ground;

Seeds with hooks that clutch and cling
Seeds I plant for flowers next spring.

Hilda I. Rostron

Ten White Snowmen

Ten white snowmen standing in a line,
One toppled over, then there were nine.

Nine white snowmen standing up straight,
One lost his balance, then there were eight.

Eight white snowmen in a snowy heaven,
The wind blew one over, then there were seven.

Seven white snowmen with pipes made of sticks,
One slumped to the ground, then there were six.

Six white snowmen standing by the drive,
One got knocked down, then there were five.

Five white snowmen outside the front door,
An icicle fell on one, then there were four.

Four white snowmen standing by the tree,
One slipped and fell apart, then there were three.

Three white snowmen underneath the yew,
One crumbled overnight, then there were two.

Two white snowmen standing in the sun,
One melted right down, then there was one.

One white snowman standing all alone,
Vanished without a trace, then there were none.

John Foster

Snowball

Mine is a comet
whistling through space
towards a distant planet.
But the planet is a head
in a woolly hat
and my snowball misses it.

Jill Townsend

From a space rocket

We looked back at the World
    rolling through Space
like a giant Moon with a calm
    cool silver face.

All its cities and countries
    had faded from sight;
all its mountains and oceans were turned
    into pure light.

Slowly, its noise and troubles
    all seemed to cease,
and the whole World was beauty and silence
    and endless peace.

Raymond Wilson

Spaceship race

Look, look,
it's the spaceship race –
Mars to Jupiter.
What a pace!
Rockets whizzing
all over the place.

Whizz whizz!
Whoosh whoosh!
One's broken down –
give it a push.

Red's in front,
Green's behind,
Blue's blown up
(never mind).

Yellow goes faster,
Green's overtaken,
Green's going to win
if I'm not mistaken.

Green's going to win –
I bet you my dinner.
Green's going to
. . . oh no!
Red is the winner.

Charles Thomson

The Old Rocking Horse

The old rocking horse
Is now worn, with no tail
And no mane. His brown paint
Is all cracked. But the course
That he rides without fail
Day and night with his quaint,
Mended smile stays the same:
There's no end to his galloping game.

John Kitching

When?

Where will you take me, magic horse,
with your mane-like wings unfurled?
Will you take me high through the midnight sky?

We'll see the world!

How will you take me, magic horse,
do you ride on a magic track?
Your shoes are gold, so I've been told . . .

They'll bring us back!

When will you take me, magic horse,
with the clover on your brow?
When shall we race through starry space?

I'll take you now!

Judith Nicholls

The Great White Horse

Have you seen the Great White Horse
    great white horse,
       great white horse?
Have you seen the great white horse
    that's carved
       upon the hill?

Have you stroked his chalky mane,
    chalky mane,
       chalky mane?
Did you let him loose again
    or leave him
       lying still?

Did you see his waking eye,
    waking eye
        waking eye –
open to the windy sky
    by day and night
        until

Buttercups grow over him
    over him
        over him:
rub him out from rim to rim
    the horse
        upon the hill!

Jean Kenward

89

Zebras

Zebras are
   horses in hiding,
shadowy
   in between strips of leaves,
watching
   for the sun-coloured
lion
   who is always hunting them.

Jill Townsend

Egg Hatch

Tiptoe
to the incubator,
try not to speak.
Listen to the tap
of a little chick's beak.

Keep very still
when you come to watch;
there's a baby chick
beginning to hatch.

First a hole
then a crack
then a cheep cheep!
Soon he'll be exploring
on his big clawed feet.

Irene Rawnsley

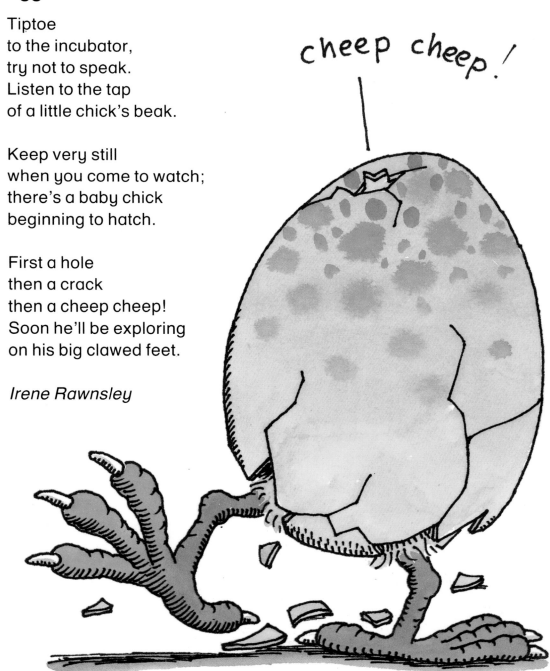

He is just a fluffy chicken

He is just a fluffy chicken.
He is only one day old.
His beak is sort of yellow.
The rest of him is gold.
'Cheep, cheep,' is all he says.
It doesn't mean a lot.
But it's all that he can utter.
It's all the speech he's got.

Finola Akister

cheep cheep!

The Nest Egg

There was once a greedy woman
who had a wonder hen.
It used to lay
a silver egg each day.
'Ho! Ho!' she thought. 'If I feed it
twice as much, it will lay me
twice as many –
oh, precious henny-penny!'
Alas, her greed was such
she gave it far too much
till, over-loaded,
the fed-up hen
exploded.

Moral:
Be content with what you've got;
Push your luck – you'll lose the lot.

Ian Serraillier

Index of first lines

Acknowledgements

The Editor and Publisher are grateful to the following for permission to include these poems:

Finola Akister, 'St George and the Dragon' © 1990 Finola Akister by permission of Frances Hall; Moira Andrew for 'The Christmas star' and 'Dear Mr Merlin' both © 1991 Moira Andrew; Tony Bradman for 'I wish I was a pirate' and 'The castle' both © 1991 Tony Bradman; Sarah Matthews for 'The Shell' © 1990 Stanley Cook, first published in *Word Houses*; John Foster for 'In the middle of the night', 'Ten White Snowmen', 'The Shadow Man', 'The Haunted House' and 'Who's Afraid?' all © 1990 John Foster and for 'The castle on the hill' and 'You little monkey!' both © 1991 John Foster; Theresa Heine for 'The mermaid' © 1991 Theresa Heine; Julie Holder for 'The Corn Scratch Kwa Kwa Hen' © 1990 Julie Holder; Martin Honeysett for 'My dad's a gorilla' © 1991 Martin Honeysett; Jean Kenward for 'Harvest' and 'The Great White Horse' both © 1990 Jean Kenward and for 'Night light' © 1991 Jean Kenward; John Kitching for 'Pebbles' and 'The Old Rocking Horse' both © 1990 John Kitching; Wendy Larmont for 'Happynessy', 'Meddling muddle', 'Reflections' and 'There was an old pirate' all © 1991 Wendy Larmont; Brian Moses for 'The Wheelchair Race' © 1990 Brian Moses; Judith Nicholls for 'Ghostly Lessons' and 'When?' both © 1990 Judith Nicholls and for 'Giant tale' and 'Look-Alike' both © 1991 Judith Nicholls; Penguin Books, Ltd. for 'He is just a fluffy chicken' from *'Before you grow up'* (Kestrel Books) © 1987 Finola Akister; Irene Rawnsley for 'At the seaside', 'Egg Hatch' and 'The Sleepy Dragon' all © 1990 Irene Rawnsley and for 'A song of sevens', 'Midnight vistors' and 'The giant visitor' all © 1991 Irene Rawnsley; Irene Rawnsley and John Foster for 'Monkey babies' © 1991 Irene Rawnsley and John Foster; The James Reeves Estate for 'The Magic Seeds' from *'The wandering moon and other poems'* (Puffin) © 1952 James Reeves; John Rice and John Foster for 'Snip the sneak' © 1991 John Rice and John Foster; John Rice for 'A Mouse in the Kitchen' from *'Rockets and Quasars'* (Aten Press) © 1984 John Rice and for 'Wanted: Smugglers' © 1991 John Rice; Clive Riche for 'Star fish' © 1991 Clive Riche; Ian Serraillier for 'The Nest Egg' © 1990 Ian Serraillier; Charles Thomson for 'Spaceship race' and 'The sea-monster's snack' both © 1991 Charles Thomson; Jill Townsend for 'Snowball' and 'Zebras' both © 1990 Jill Townsend; Raymond Wilson for 'The Fox and the Crow' © 1990 Raymond Wilson and for 'From a space rocket' © 1991 Raymond Wilson; Irene Yates for 'Harvest Festival' from Infant Projects No 60 (Scholastic) © 1988 Irene Yates and for 'The Flying Reptiles Race' © 1990 Irene Yates.

Although every effort has been made to contact the owners of copyright material, a few have been impossible to trace, but if they contact the Publisher, correct acknowledgement will be made in future editions.